The Secrets of a High-Value Man.

Discover How to Become a Man of Purpose, Dignity, and Strength.

Harry. M. Cleveland.

<u>**DEDICATION**</u>

I dedicate this book to my family. Your constant love and support have been my rock on this journey. Your encouragement lights my way, and this accomplishment is as much yours as it is mine. Thank you for always believing in me.

TABLE OF CONTENTS

INTRODUCTION

Among other struggles in life, a man is

trying to get his life together, standing against the odds of failure, and doing whatever it takes to survive. This life is all rosy, some ups and downs and things make you want to doubt the reason for your existence but the truth of the matter is that you are doing all it takes and there is always light at the end of the tunnel.

This book is made to encourage all men out there trying to do their very best. It expresses the sweetness and pain of becoming a man. Through everything a man goes through, from being a boy to being a man and a father. The journey is not easy, that is why all men must be celebrated.

Working 9-5 with a miniature pay and still finding a way to cater to the family. He pays tuition, house rent, mortgage, water bill, medical bills, and many other bills to be paid yet he doesn't complain about it, he carries his responsibility with pride and cares for his family even more.

Ps: I wouldn't have written this book if I had not had my personal experience being a man or had faced similar challenges. I dedicated my time and effort to making this book to encourage and help men out there struggling to find purpose and balance in life. This book will be your guide to achieving the life you want. The knowledge you will get from this book is worth more than the price of the book. READ AND IMPLEMENT!

CHAPTER 1

NO ONE GIVES A FUCK!

If you want something you have to allocate time to do it. That is discipline, you have to work when you don't feel like working. Life is hard but it's what makes it beautiful, knowing that all you got, you worked hard for it and you're proud of yourself.

Life's not friendly to men, almost everything that comes your way has to be through defeat, war, and pain.

It's a war for money,

War for love,

War for acceptance,

War for domination,

War to have a happy ending,

There's almost nothing a man doesn't struggle for. As a man, you have to build yourself to a point where you can't be brought down. No man should be depressed. Depression is only an excuse for laziness and failure. Life is depressing but it is your responsibility not to let it affect you as a man instead channel what you feel into building the life you want.

No law says you should be happy all the time. Life is not a bed of roses, you will feel pain, you will want to give up, and you'll question the reason for your existence, but DON'T YOU DARE FORGET THE REASON YOU STARTED? If the reason isn't valuable any longer, look for a new reason. There is no gain in quitting.

You can survive even if you're miserable, refuse to be a baby, and chicken away from problems. Stand up tall and face them head-on. You have to act differently from the way you feel, that is one of the rules of masculinity. Look into the lives of successful men and notice that none of them ever got to where they are now by letting emotions and fear lead them.

Women get afraid and they run.

Children get afraid and they run.

 But you as a man can also get afraid but you STAND!

Take, for instance, a raccoon that runs into your living room with your wife and kids in it... you know what will happen right?

Yes, of course, your wife and kids will run in fear living you there. Your wife would even carry the kids on her in split seconds but not you. They didn't do this because they love you less, but because of the automatic dominance that comes with being a man.

Imagine if you ran away in fear with them.

They won't see you the same way again and that is for sure. I'm not going to sugarcoat things.

I didn't say they won't love you, but they won't see you the same way again. And the next time you might want to brag about being strong and mighty, even your kids would remind you of the time you ran away because of a raccoon.

But if you show dominance and chase the raccoon away to protect your family, you'll earn more trust and faith in your family. That's the same with life as a man, shy away from problems you will end up losing your value. Trust me, you're as good as dead when you've lost your value as a man.

Men have always been respected for bravery. Bravery is on the other hand of fear and it is what will build you and it will reflect who you are when a woman looks into your eyes-- she can tell if she's safe or not. It is what people in general see when they look at you.

Everything is your responsibility,

To become the best,

To be at the top,

To be successful,

To be of value,

To be above your competitors,

You cannot achieve this by talking it into existence, anyone who tells you this is lying to you. You need to live it into existence. Challenge yourself to do the things that seem naturally hard and watch yourself excel in them. You need to go out there and do things that are genuinely stressful, difficult, and almost impossible to do. That's why you need to take responsibility for your actions. The decisions you make today will shape and design you into the man you will become. Life is hard, and being a man is hard, but how you shape yourself will determine how difficult things will be for you.

Take responsibility for the information you consume and how you work with it.

Is it building you?

Is it keeping you in the past?

Is it depriving you of the joy you're supposed to feel?

Take note of all these, answer them, and know if you should hold on to that information or let go of it.

There is no easy life for you as a man, you have to pay a price for everything you do

There's no easy life for you as a man. All the pain and sadness you feel, it's all because you're a man. If you were a woman you wouldn't be facing that share of pain. You can either accept the trauma that comes with being a man of value or suffer in life as a nobody. Value is priceless— in life, you have to run for it with all you have otherwise it'll be taken away from you.

Nobody cares about you;

Nobody gives a fuck!

When you don't make a mark on the wall, it's almost as if you don't exist.

Do you want to live in obscurity? Where everything is effortless and painless?

If you answered yes to that, then you still have a long way to go and a mind to rebuild.

If you live in obscurity, you'll live in regret. Yes, you read right. Obscurity leads to regrets. Regrets of knowing that you'd have achieved better if you tried harder. Regrets of seeing others succeed but not you. Regrets of your gem but not being able to carry it. It's painful, you don't want to live like that.

Here's a question for you;

 Choose between one

A. A Life of invisibility with a lower rent bill?

B. A life where you conquered your fears and worked hard to make sure that the rent was paid?

Nothing in life is free, everything you get, you have to pay rent for it. The choice you make is yours and you must be extremely dedicated to making life work for you. You must accept the decision you make and accept that everything is your fault. You must do what's right because. It's your duty and yours alone not because you benefit from it. That's what life has placed on you.

One good thing about life is that you get exactly what you give. You see men who work hard, eat the right food, and wear nice clothes coming out looking super attractive. That's not luck, they worked for it, and they gave out their time and effort. Also, you see people who dedicate 4-5 hours of their day just to learn a course on business management, travel the world to get high-class knowledge, read books, and ditch whatever will jeopardize their vision. These people GAVE! You must give something to life to get something back in return. The amazing part of it is that what you give, isn't going to cost you anything but your willingness.

CHAPTER 2

BUILDING A
HIGH-VALUE MAN

A typical guy who decided to change the way
he lived and develop into a high-value man. He
began by boosting his self-assurance. He
discovered how to accept himself, flaws and all,
as opposed to being overly critical of himself.
He accepted his individuality and discovered
people were drawn to his genuine assurance.

He worked hard to hone his communication
abilities. He engaged in active listening, giving
people a sense of worth and hearing. He carried
on interesting talks and posed smart questions.
People valued his sincere attention, and he
developed strong bonds with friends, family,
and coworkers.

One more thing he concentrated on was emotional intelligence. He gained the ability to properly control his emotions and relate to other people. He offered more than just advice when his friend was struggling; he also lent a sympathetic ear and offered emotional support. His friend gained comfort and increased appreciation for their friendship.

He is also aware of the value of ongoing self-development. He studied books, went to workshops, and engaged in activities that challenged his thinking. He spent money on his education and development as a person, which made him an informed and engaging company. All admired his curiosity for learning and conversational versatility.

He paid extra care to his bodily well-being as well as his mental and emotional state. He followed a healthy diet, worked out frequently, and put sleep first. He felt terrific and others wanted to be near him because of his vigor and excitement. His discipline and respect for himself were demonstrated by his healthy living choices, which motivated everyone around him.

He had a strong sense of compassion and altruism. He assisted the less fortunate by volunteering at a neighborhood charity. His acts of compassion and goodwill not only improved the lives of others around him but also enhanced his own. He felt satisfaction in having a beneficial effect on the world, and because of his selflessness, he was well-liked in his neighborhood.

He was a high-value man, ambitious, and focused on his objectives. He was devoted and tenacious in his pursuit of his interests. He persisted in the face of obstacles, and his tenacity motivated others to follow their aspirations as well. His success was also judged by the beneficial impact he had on those around him, not only in terms of money.

Masculinity isn't just about having a beard or being strong. It's more like a set of qualities and behaviors that society often expects from men. Things like being tough, confident, and independent. The toxic thing about masculinity is the lack of it.

Believe it or not, men do get scared. They might fear not being good enough, not being strong enough, or not being able to protect their loved ones. Sometimes, they worry about not fitting into the idea of what a "real man" should be. These fears can be pretty overwhelming. Life throws challenges at everyone, and men are no exception. They face pressure to succeed in their careers, provide for their families, and always be emotionally strong.

As a man, there is a certain level of uncertainty you are allowed to face, regardless of how the world displays it. You are not allowed to feel pain for too long. Let that shit go, you are worth more than that. There is a need for an upright man, nobody wants a loser. The world needs men, with well-built egos and uprightness and you can only be one by being a high-value man.

There is more to becoming a high-value man than simply having cash or attractive physical characteristics. It's about developing the traits and abilities that help you become a complete, well-liked, and powerful person. Whatever is attractive to you and anyone you come across is the standard you set for yourself. Physical appearance matters and I'm not talking about height, complexion, or size. The way you portray yourself as a man will determine the physical outlook people will get when they see you. As a man, you should carry yourself in the way you speak, walk, and engage in conversation, to do this, you MUST learn how to;

Speak

Be funny

Order meals appropriately

Dress

Handle women

Get things done

Get the right accessory

Get a good haircut

Maintain good oral health

Communicate.

Be gentle.

Be polite.

These may not be all but it is a good way to start. You may not know but a lot of people are watching. Being a high-value man is to be almost perfect by default. I said "almost" because nobody is perfect. No one loves men who jump to conclusions. As a high-value man, think before you act, before you talk, and consider what may be the outcome of the decision you make and how it affects you. That does not include general life alone. It includes the decisions you make about money, sex, who to spend the rest of your life with, what to invest in, and what not to. All these and many more count to what makes you a high-value man. Matter of fact, if you flop in these areas, you will regret it big time.

If you think something is garbage, be it women, work, or people, it's your fault. Yes, you read right. Everything should be your fault as a man.

You walk into a store and say, "Shit, this place is a mess"

It's your fault for being in that messy store

Or you say, "Damn, their customer service is bad"

It's your fault for not being in a place with better customer service.

You meet a girl and complain about her not being up to your standard, it's your fault for not attracting a high-value woman. High-value men attract high-value women. In general, high-value men attract high-value things.

Great stores

Great women,

Great hotels,

First-class service.

There is no other way around it. Always find a way to make things your fault, it gives you an edge over your situation and activates your mind for a fast and better solution.

If you don't stay at the top, you are not worthy to be competed against. There is no class, vision, or goal, anyone would see and want to imitate. High-value men love good competition, and you shouldn't be around competition if you want to be a high-value man. You have to always wake up and look yourself in the mirror and say "I am the man".

You're not unlucky with business, women, career, money, and personal development. you've not built yourself to face the shit that people who you think are "lucky" have faced. You fill yourself with depression, anxiety, pain, bitterness, hatred, laziness, and every form of worthless excuse you use to withdraw from being the man you're supposed to be.

How can you feel depressed if you've got the business of your dreams?

How can you feel depressed if you're with the hottest girl in town?

How can you feel depressed if you make millions and billions of dollars a month?

How can you feel depressed if you own the most expensive car?

How can you feel depressed if you own the most expensive house?

How can you feel depressed if you've got a beautiful family?

So many questions to ask because depression, anxiety, and laziness are just excuses for a man who is afraid to get shit done. I previously mentioned how high-value men attract high-value things. If you're not a high-value man, you can't attract any of these.

As a man you have to understand that it's always a constant competition for you. Whatever it is you want, someone else wants it and is making a tireless effort to get it, see why you have to work your ass out and face every challenge head-on because someone out there is doing all it takes to get what you want.

If the world is that competitive, what excuse do you have to be depressed?

Get up, man!

Get your act together!

Get your shit together!

Work like a beast!

you've got so much to prove to the world so don't get tired now.

Being aware of your thoughts and feelings can help you understand and respond to situations better. "Winning starts from the mind" Learn to control your mind, accept things that are helpful for your growth and improvement, and reject things that are not. Set goals that align with your growth and vision. You have no excuse for stagnation. Everything you need to succeed has been made available to you, you just have to be willing to learn and accept it. You can control your mind, so do it correctly.

Because it results in a rewarding life, being a high-value man is worthwhile. You'll make a difference in your community, gain the respect of people, and have important relationships. You can become a person of tremendous value by embracing traits like self-assurance, emotional intelligence, ongoing self-improvement, physical health, compassion, and ambition. It's not just about enticing people; it's also about improving yourself and making a positive impact on the world.

You have to demonstrate respect and integrity as someone who consistently treats others with courtesy and fairness. keep their promises, be truthful and open in communication, and empathize with others. Take responsibility for your actions, don't blame anyone for the things you get yourself into.

CHAPTER 3
GET ASSETS

Being financially stable and having financial intelligence are two different things. We know that assets are things that are utilized to produce monetary value. When you focus more on assets than liabilities, you set yourself up for life. Assets are long-term investment plans. Investment is anything that brings a return after a while on an initial payment.

If you were not taught how to invest and save in school, then you know yourself that education. There are so many books you can read, and information is littered everywhere, on the internet, on Twitter (now X), YouTube, Quora, Google, and Medium. You owe yourself the responsibility of utilizing these platforms.

"Did you know that the greatest asset you can get is information and knowledge?"

This is because once you have acquired information and knowledge you can use it your for benefit over and over again. Imagine if you have knowledge about trading and you're a pro in it when you've let people know about your expertise, and you begin to offer it as a service to people whether directly or indirectly, you charge $500 or more for a private coaching or better still, you create a course on it and decide to put it out for sale. People will contact you on this offer, let's assume you're being contacted by 10 persons per week

$$10 \times 500 = \$5,000$$

that's how much you make for yourself in a week.

See why knowledge and information are an asset?

By definition, An asset is any possession owned by a person, company, or nation that holds the potential to be utilized or traded for generating advantages, in the future.

It does not have to be trading alone, it could be anything at all as long as it brings you money. A skill is an asset.

When you buy stocks, shares, or bonds, you're essentially getting assets. Think of assets like valuable things you own. Let's take stocks, for example. Owning stocks means you own a piece of a company. Over time, the company might give you money called dividends, or the value of your stocks can go up, called capital gains.

Now, imagine having a property. By owning it, you can make money through rental income. Plus, if you decide to sell it later, you might make a big profit. Whether it's stocks or property, you need to have something valuable that can bring you money in different ways. As a man, you need to sustain yourself with multiple sources of income. Don't listen to anyone who tells you to rely on one source of income regardless of the million dollars you make out of that particular source. The wealthiest men on Earth never settled for one income stream. Besides stocks and properties, they might invest in - Business Ventures, Entrepreneurship, Real Estate Investments,

Venture Capital, Intellectual Property, Private Equity, Cryptocurrency and Alternative Investments.

Do you think they don't have good reasons for doing this?

You can't survive on one source of income. You risk even more by depending on one source.

What if it fails?

Have you considered the risk exposure?

Have you considered how it will limit your overall financial growth potential?

Did you know it can lead to financial instability and difficulties in meeting financial obligations?

These and many more are the outcomes of putting all your financial eggs in one basket. As a man building his life for a better future, learn to diversify.

Having these assets is like planting seeds in a garden of financial strength. When you grab stocks, it's like saying, "I'm in on this company's success." Just like a well-tended garden gives you fruits, these stocks can give you dividends – a steady flow of extra money. It's a bit like the reward for taking good care of your garden.

Now, why does this matter?

Well, those dividends aren't just pocket change. They make your money situation steady and reliable. Plus, having these assets opens doors for more opportunities. It's like the garden growing more and more, offering you chances to plant new seeds (make more investments) and watch them grow too.

So, having assets isn't just about having random stuff; it's like building a strong, growing garden of money that gives you stability and a way to make even more money over time.

Think about someone starting their own business – that's an entrepreneur. They're not just earning money; they're like creators in the money world. These business ventures can grow into something big, bringing in lots of money and encouraging new ideas and financial freedom.

Now, having things that make money (assets) isn't just about having cash. It's like having the power to make choices. It lets you do what you want in the long run. A mix of different money-makers gives you flexibility. It allows you to have different options – trying new things, facing tough times, or leaving a legacy for the next generation and the power to decide your money story.

CHAPTER 4

BUILD PURPOSE AND PASSION

Life is like a big adventure, and finding your purpose and passion is like discovering your special treasure map. For you as a man, it's about figuring out what makes you happy, where your peace comes from, and the things that no matter the circumstances, you will always fall back to.

Your purpose is what guides you and gives your journey a sense of direction. To find it, you need to take a good look inside yourself, think about what you are good at, what you care about, and what dreams make you smile - it's like finding the heart of your own story.

It's not just liking something; it's loving it so much that you can't get enough. Whether it's a

job, a hobby, or something you believe in, your
family, your dreams, goals, and aspirations.
Passion keeps you going, even when things get
tough. It's the spark that turns ordinary
moments into awesome adventures. When you
bring purpose and passion together, you create
a superpower combo.

The greatest mistake you can make for yourself
is not being able to buy the most expensive cars,
or houses or own a million-dollar company. It is
living a life without purpose. Having purpose
challenges you to achieve your big dreams.
Without purpose, life has no meaning.

I used to be just a regular guy with a
not-so-regular obsession – you know, cookies,
cakes, all the good stuff. But life wasn't always a
piece of cake for me.

I had this big dream of opening a bakery.
Sounds cool, right? But everyone around me
said it was a bad idea.

"Stick to your regular job," they'd say.

It made me feel kinda down, but I just couldn't let go of my love for baking.

Life got tough. Bills piled up, and my dream seemed far away. But here's the thing: those tough times made me love baking even more. It wasn't just a fun hobby; it became super important to me.

Even when things went wrong – ovens breaking, cakes falling – I didn't give up. I started believing in myself, even when others didn't. I saved money, borrowed a bit, and finally opened my bakery.

And you know what?

People loved it! My bakery became this awesome place where everyone got tasty treats. It wasn't about being perfect; it was about learning and getting better.

Life can be tricky, but you can turn things around. Believe in yourself, even if others don't. I opened one of the best bakeries not because it was easy, but because I felt deep down it was what I was supposed to do. And that is purpose and passion for you.

The journey of life is not easy, but before you embark on this journey, you must fill yourself with the right reasons, energy, and fuel to keep you going. If you don't, it will be bad for the man you want to become. Think ahead of time, and consider the outcome the efforts you put in now will yield.

You need something to keep you going during the tough days.

The tough days that come when you no longer see a reason to pursue your dreams.

The tough days that come when the energy you started with seems to be missing.

Everyone is faced with challenges sometimes, but it is their passion and purpose that reminds them of the reason they started. Your purpose and passion make you persevere against all odds. When others quit, you stand tall and say,

"This is my purpose, my journey, my passion and I will carry it with everything I've got".

The good things in life won't come knocking at your doorstep. You need to put in the grind, power, and sacrifice. Nobody is going to do it but you.

You have to say,

"This is what I want"

"This is what I'm going to"

"Nobody will tell me otherwise"

"I have set my mind to it, I'm going to achieve it"

Have you seen why you need a purpose?

You must live the life you deserve. To know what you want is not enough, but to strive and dedicate your sweat and tears to achieve what you want.